*Greater Than a [illegible]
available in Ebook and Audiobook format.

Greater Than a Tourist Book Series
Reviews from Readers

I think the series is wonderful and beneficial for tourists to get information before visiting the city.

-Seckin Zumbul, Izmir Turkey

I am a world traveler who has read many trip guides but this one really made a difference for me. I would call it a heartfelt creation of a local guide expert instead of just a guide.

-Susy, Isla Holbox, Mexico

New to the area like me, this is a must have!

-Joe, Bloomington, USA

This is a good series that gets down to it when looking for things to do at your destination without having to read a novel for just a few ideas.

-Rachel, Monterey, USA

Good information to have to plan my trip to this destination.

-Pennie Farrell, Mexico

Great ideas for a port day.

-Mary Martin USA

Aptly titled, you won't just be a tourist after reading this book. You'll be greater than a tourist!

-Alan Warner, Grand Rapids, USA

Even though I only have three days to spend in San Miguel in an upcoming visit, I will use the author's suggestions to guide some of my time there. An easy read - with chapters named to guide me in directions I want to go.

-Robert Catapano, USA

Great insights from a local perspective! Useful information and a very good value!

-Sarah, USA

This series provides an in-depth experience through the eyes of a local. Reading these series will help you to travel the city in with confidence and it'll make your journey a unique one.

-Andrew Teoh, Ipoh, Malaysia

GREATER THAN A TOURIST- ANNAPOLIS MARYLAND USA

50 Travel Tips from a Local

L. Elizabeth Forry

First Edition
Cover designed by: Ivana Stamenkovic
Cover Image: https://pixabay.com/photos/annapolis-city-dock-bay-ships-5183927/

Image 1: By Diiscool - Own work, CC0, https://commons.wikimedia.org/w/index.php?curid=24514777
Image 2: By Photograph by D Ramey Logan, CC BY 4.0, https://commons.wikimedia.org/w/index.php?curid=41445571
Image 3: By Rdsmith4 - Own work, CC BY-SA 2.5, https://commons.wikimedia.org/w/index.php?curid=28061
Image 4: By Smallbones - Own work, Public Domain, https://commons.wikimedia.org/w/index.php?curid=11263238

CZYK Publishing Since 2011.
Greater Than a Tourist

Lock Haven, PA

ISBN: 9798662862159

>TOURIST

50 TRAVEL TIPS FROM A LOCAL

BOOK DESCRIPTION

With travel tips and culture in our guidebooks written by a local, it is never too late to visit Annapolis. Greater Than a Tourist- *Annapolis, Maryland, United States* by Author *L. Elizabeth Forry* offers the inside scoop on the city of Annapolis, the Sailing Capital of the World. Most travel books tell you how to travel like a tourist. Although there is nothing wrong with that, as part of the 'Greater Than a Tourist' series, this book will give you candid travel tips from someone who has lived at your next travel destination. This guide book will not tell you exact addresses or store hours but instead gives you knowledge that you may not find in other smaller print travel books. Experience cultural, culinary delights, and attractions with the guidance of a Local. Slow down and get to know the people with this invaluable guide. By the time you finish this book, you will be eager and prepared to discover new activities at your next travel destination.

Inside this travel guide book you will find:

Visitor information from a Local
Tour ideas and inspiration
Save time with valuable guidebook information

Greater Than a Tourist- A Travel Guidebook with 50 Travel Tips from a Local. Slow down, stay in one place, and get to know the people and culture. By the time you finish this book, you will be eager and prepared to travel to your next destination.

OUR STORY

Traveling is a passion of the Greater than a Tourist book series creator. Lisa studied abroad in college, and for their honeymoon Lisa and her husband toured Europe. During her travels to Malta, an older man tried to give her some advice based on his own experience living on the island since he was a young boy. She was not sure if she should talk to the stranger but was interested in his advice. When traveling to some places she was wary to talk to locals because she was afraid that they weren't being genuine. Through her travels, Lisa learned how much locals had to share with tourists. Lisa created the Greater Than a Tourist book series to help connect people with locals. A topic that locals are very passionate about sharing.

TABLE OF CONTENTS

13. Trivia Night
14. Casinos
15. The Maryland Renaissance Festival

Shopping & Fun!
16. A Potter's Delight
17. Books Glorious Books
18. Annapolis Town Center
19. Westfield Annapolis
20. Annapolis Harbor Center

Tours & Crawls
21. Pirate Boat Tours
22. Ghost Tours
23. Historical Tours
24. Pub Crawls & Food Tours

Points Beyond Annapolis
25. Count De Rochambeau House
26. Historic London Town and Gardens
27. Sandy Point Park
28. The Bay Bridge

Unique Spots
29. Graul's Grocery
30. Designated Historical Houses

DEDICATION

This book is dedicated to Mom, My Joe, such devoted sisters Cherie & Lauren, my amazing Annapolis tribe who welcomed my open-armed and my boys Ewan & Finnegan.

ABOUT THE AUTHOR

L. Elizabeth Forry is a mother, writer, educator, blogger, and actor who resides just outside of Annapolis, Maryland. She settled in Annapolis after spending time living in Washington, D.C., and Chicago to be closer to her family. She wanted a more suburban-like setting that held the old-world city charm, that she loves so much in America's oldest cities.

After receiving her B.A. in English/Theater and B.A. in Music from Lebanon Valley College, she moved to Japan for a year to teach English.

Upon her return to the states, she began her career in early childhood education. She received an M.S. in ECE from the University of North Dakota. She spent fourteen years working as a teacher in Washington, D.C., Chicago and Maryland before committing to writing full time.

Travelling is one of her favorite pastimes; her favorite places include Paris, Rome, Savannah, Dublin, New York City, and Disney World.

She spent two years living in Annapolis before purchasing a home with her partner Joe about fifteen minutes outside the city. She is often strolling the streets of Annapolis with coffee in her hand while browsing through the shops and bookstores or sitting on the waterfront watching the boats. She has even been seen a few times performing on the Colonial Players stage, one of the oldest theater companies in the state.

She spends her time reading fiction, memoirs, and travel guides and is always planning the next trip, even the ones that are not going to happen! She enjoys crosswords, puzzles, local sightseeing and writing for her parenting and mom-life blog elizabethforry.com

HOW TO USE THIS BOOK

The *Greater Than a Tourist* book series was written by someone who has lived in an area for over three months. The goal of this book is to help travelers either dream or experience different locations by providing opinions from a local. The author has made suggestions based on their own experiences. Please check before traveling to the area in case the suggested places are unavailable.

Travel Advisories: As a first step in planning any trip abroad, check the Travel Advisories for your intended destination.
https://travel.state.gov/content/travel/en/traveladvisories/traveladvisories.html

FROM THE PUBLISHER

Traveling can be one of the most important parts of a person's life. The anticipation and memories that you have are some of the best. As a publisher of the Greater Than a Tourist, as well as the popular *50 Things to Know* book series, we strive to help you learn about new places, spark your imagination, and inspire you. Wherever you are and whatever you do I wish you safe, fun, and inspiring travel.

Lisa Rusczyk Ed. D.
CZYK Publishing

WELCOME TO > TOURIST

Aerial view of Annapolis, Maryland, Chesapeake Bay, and Chesapeake Bay Bridge

View into City Dock with Market House at right and Main Street to left

Over Annapolis Harbor & Dock Street

Downtown Annapolis's Main Street in September 2004

"The world is a book, and those who do not travel read only one page."

-Augustine of Hippo

Annapolis is the city that time forgot. One can lose themselves in time wandering the old streets and seeing buildings built before America was a country. It is possible to find a quiet corner or bench to take in the landscape and architecture lose yourself in time. As you sit, you can almost see Alexander Hamilton or George Washington walking these streets. While visiting, you can stand in the room where Washington resigned his military commission in 1783. Annapolis is a popular tourist destination for U.S. citizens and overseas travelers, receiving millions of visitors each year. There is truly no wrong time of year to visit. In the summer and spring, you can experience sailing, water sports, and festivals. Fall brings beautiful foliage, outdoor dining, and Halloween pub crawls and parties. Winter is a delight with Christmas shopping, colonial carolers, and the annual boat light parade. Annapolis offers the best of the tourist industry all year long. American History, delicious cuisine, a thriving arts scene and sailing and boating events are just a few of the reasons to visit. With so much to do and see in and around Annapolis, it is one of America's hidden travel gems.

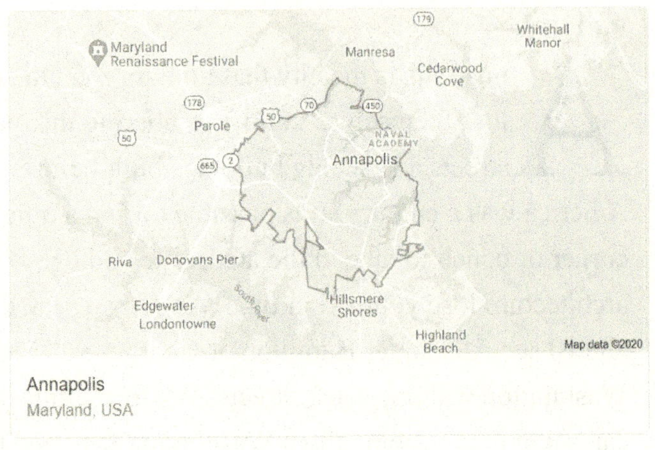

Annapolis
Maryland, USA

Annapolis Maryland Climate

	High	Low
January	45	30
February	47	31
March	54	37
April	67	48
May	74	58
June	83	67
July	87	72
August	85	71
September	79	65
October	69	53
November	58	42
December	49	35

GreaterThanaTourist.com

Temperatures are in Fahrenheit degrees.
Source: NOAA

ANNAPOLIS HIGHLIGHTS

1. A WALK THROUGH HISTORY

Annapolis is a walking city. The streets are narrow and often one-way, which can make driving complicated, especially if you are not familiar with the area nor sure where you are headed. Driving issues aside, walking is the best way to get a feel for the city. I recommend looking up a self-guided walking tour, or simply wander around and see what you can discover. There are historical treasures all over downtown, not to mention, you will get to see some of the beautiful homes. You will want to pack comfortable walking shoes to avoid blisters. Many of the sidewalks and roads are brick and uneven. There are some steep hills as the city gravitates naturally downward towards the water.

2. THE HARBOR

The harbor in Annapolis is the epicenter of downtown. Ego Alley is a beautiful place to sit and watch the yachts and boats on the water. I enjoy sitting there with an iced coffee on a beautiful sunny day. The harbor is also a pleasant place to walk around and get some exercise. You can rent small boats, kayaks, and paddle boats from vendors or take a sailing class at the Annapolis Sailing School. Often, dog walkers galore are down by the water, so if you have brought your four-legged friend with you on vacation, feel free to roam around! Annapolis LOVES dogs. You are also likely to see musicians ranging from opera singers to jazz guitarists, to hip hop dancers down and around the harbor.

3. MARYLAND STATE HOUSE

The Maryland State House was built in 1779 and played a pivotal role in many events during the American Revolution. It is still used today as the meeting place for The Maryland General assembly. It was designated a historical site in 1960. The State House is open to the public for free most days unless it is used for business purposes. One of the highlights of this historical site is being able to stand in the room George Washington resigned his military commission in 1793. The Treaty of Paris was ratified in this building marking the official end to the Revolutionary War. You can see his personal copy of his resignation speech on display, which was acquired by the State Archives in 2007. The Maryland State House served as the first capitol building in the United States, housing the continental congress from November 26, 1783, to August 13, 1784. The wooden dome atop the building was completed in 1794 and is the oldest wooden dome of its kind in the United States.

4. NAVAL ACADEMY

The United States Naval Academy is situated in downtown Annapolis. It is the home to many significant events throughout the year, including visits from the president and other major politicians. The Blue Angel flyovers are always fantastic to experience. If you have small children and are planning to witness a Blue Angel demo be warned, it is deafening and is likely to frighten them. Visitors are allowed on the grounds of The Naval Academy in limited areas; however, all adults 21 and older must have a valid I.D. compliant with the REAL ID Act. Individuals will go through a security checkpoint, and no weapons of any kind will be permitted onto the property. Those with active or retired military I.D. are allowed to enter through a different checkpoint and may drive onto the grounds to park. I suggest you visit their page and view the guidelines before visiting. A big draw each fall is the Navy football games. I have been stuck in traffic many a time due to it being game day! Commissioning Week also draws huge crowds and a sense of celebration. It is always a delight to see all the young men and women walking about the city in their dress whites.

5. WEST STREET

West street is the other central hub after Main Street. There are many bars and restaurants here. In my opinion, West Street is home to the best restaurant in Annapolis, Level: A Small Plated Lounge. For further information on Level, please view the restaurant section. West Street is where you'll find the only Dunkin Donuts downtown, so if you need your Dunkin fix this is the place to go! West Street is one route to follow to take you directly out of center into the remainder of Annapolis. West Street is also one of the few places in Annapolis to stay in a mainstream hotel. The Hilton Garden Inn offers clean, modern-style rooms with all the amenities typically included with that lodging class. It also provides free parking for guests, which is excellent since parking can be hard to come by downtown.

6. QUIET WATERS PARK

In an expansive park set outside of downtown Annapolis, Quiet Waters is a great place to escape from the busy streets of downtown. Set on 340 acres of land, it offers several amenities, depending on the time of year that ranges from paddleboats to an outdoor ice-skating rink. There are 6 miles of paved hiking trails and an excellent multi-level playground for the kids that looks like a castle with turrets. The park is dog friendly and provides a specific dog beach area. Quiet Waters in itself is a significant tourist attraction with close to a million people a year visiting. You have to pay to park if you are not a member, but it is a nominal fee used for the park's upkeep. It is a per car charge. The official entrance for the park is 600 Quiet Waters Park Road.

7. WAR MEMORIALS

On the grounds of St. John's College are two war memorials placed by alumni in honor of fellow alumni who have died in service. One was set in 1920 to honor those who served in WWI, and one was placed in the 90s to honor all former sacrifices by fellow alumni. There is a replica of The Liberty Bell, created by the same foundry, but missing the iconic crack! Maryland's WWII Memorial, dedicated in 1998, stands on the 450 median and overlooks the Naval Academy. It is designed in an amphitheater-style with 48 stone columns designating the 48 states at the time of WWII.

8. CARROLL HOUSE & GARDENS

Flowers and a beautiful colonial estate house sitting on the water make this an excellent place to tour on a beautiful day. Charles Carroll was one of the signers of the Declaration of Independence and has a nearby county named after him! His family lived in the home for four generations. Public tours of the house are performed daily between 12 pm and 4 pm from June to October. Admission is free for groups of 6 or less. A private tour can be arranged for a fee of $5 per person.

9. ST. MARY'S CATHOLIC CHURCH & GARDEN

Adjacent to the Carroll House sits St. Mary's Catholic Church and gardens. The gardens are a beautiful place to rest and take in some beauty. Set in a quiet corner, one can quickly lose themselves in thought. The land for the church was given to the parish in 1852 by 4 of Charles Carroll's granddaughters; he was the only Catholic signer of the Declaration of Independence. If you wish to worship at the church during your stay, their website offers various service and devotion times.

LIVE ENTERTAINMENT

10. A PLAY'S THE THING

The theater is alive and thriving in the Annapolis area. Downtown Annapolis is host to two long-running theater companies. The Colonial Players run a yearlong season, mostly plays, and is one of the oldest theater companies in Maryland. Their cozy and intimate theater is situated in the round providing a unique view to any performance you see there. It is one of the few places you can go and say, "not a bad seat in the house.". Down by the harbor is Annapolis Summer Garden Theater, another long-standing staple. They run three blockbuster musicals a summer in their beautiful outdoor theater. Be warned they often sell out well before the season starts. Since the theater is situated outdoors, shows can be canceled due to heavy rain or storms. It can also be hot and humid, which is why they perform in the evenings only. Nearby is 2nd Star Productions in Bowie, MD. Hosted in an old barn converted theater, they put on top-rated musicals on their beautiful proscenium style stage. Their season typically includes one play as well. Seating is first come first served, and since the audience slants downwards, I recommend sitting towards the back. Stage and Screen Studios in Millersville, houses children, acted productions that are put on after the children go through and learn about the audition and performance process in a 12-16-week workshop. They incorporate modern graphics and lighting with their giant white screen as a backdrop. Their productions can be an entertaining experience for young children to watch. Stage and Screen also frequently houses The Pasadena Theater Company, another long-standing company in the area. They produce smaller-scale productions with top-rate talent. I have personally performed with two of these companies!

11. LIVE MUSIC GALORE

Downtown Annapolis is a fantastic spot to catch live music. Many up and coming bands play with no cover charge, and some venues host some well-known performers with a ticketed entrance. Ram's Head on Stage, located on West Street, is one of the best places to go for a night out. Casey Abrams, KT Tunstall, and David Crosby are just a few of the names who have performed here. In addition to exceptional music, they offer an extensive draft and bottled selection. On Maryland Ave, Galway Bay is a favorite of mine for Irish music and good beer. It can be crowded in the bar, but it's a fun and lively crowd. About 15 minutes north of Annapolis in Severna Park, Brian Boru is another place I frequent for authentic Irish food and great live music. Live music is held on Friday and Saturday nights. You can either sit in the bar and watch the performance or enjoy one of their cozy booths and simply listen as you enjoy your meal. 49 West Café, their name is their address, is a delightful cozy coffee shop/bar that often hosts live music. They have a backroom that typically requires a cover charge, but they also host musicians in the main café free of charge. If you decide to stop in here, check out the dessert case! Bonus, the artwork hanging along their walls, is for sale!

12. IT'S A GRAND NIGHT FOR SINGING

For those of you who love singing or watching Karaoke, the Annapolis area is a hot spot. With a thriving music and theater scene, most places you go tend to have top-quality talent, making the night much more enjoyable. However, have no fear; if you cannot hold a tune, you will still receive copious support in the venues mentioned here. If you would like to stay downtown, then I recommend Dock Street Bar & Grill. This hot spot is right on the water and offers excellent food. Karaoke held Saturday nights. If you want the water view but want to get out of the downtown area, head to The Jetty just on the other side of the Bay Bridge. They offer fresh crabs and stunning views of the Chesapeake Bay. It can get crowded, and the rotation can be long, but there is plenty of outdoor space to hang out. Karaoke is Thursday nights. My personal hang out is at Ellie's

Bar & Grill north of Annapolis in Millersville. A much more subdued atmosphere with a great and friendly bar staff. Ellie's is the place to head if you are looking for some classic rock, country, and show tunes! Karaoke is held every Monday and three Saturdays each month. One Saturday, a month is reserved for a live band, and the schedule can vary, so I recommend calling ahead. I know two of the K.J.'s personally, and I guarantee wherever you go, you will have a great time!

13. TRIVIA NIGHT

Trivia Night lovers have plenty of options to choose from in the Annapolis area. Ellie's Bar & Grill 15 minutes northwest of downtown hosts a lively trivia night on Thursdays. Get there early and register your team, or they may run out of space! Union Jacks at the Annapolis Town Center is an English Style pub that holds Trivia every Tuesday at 8 pm. They require advanced registration, and you can do so online. In addition to offering fantastic and delicious food, they host a terrific beer, wine, and drink menu. Castlebay Irish Pub in downtown Annapolis is another option for great food and a great trivia night; check their website for dates and times. West End Grill is a second option for downtown trivia; it is hosted on Wednesday nights by Charm City Trivia. Plenty of additional options abound as Annapolis is no stranger to bars and pubs. The website Chesapeake Family Life lists several other trivia night options.

14. CASINOS

Gambling lovers rejoice, there are two fantastic Casinos not far from Annapolis. First, is the Horseshoe Casino, located right as you begin to enter downtown Baltimore, a mere 30-minute drive from Annapolis. It is home to three celebrity chef restaurants, one of those being Ramsay Steak. The Horseshoe Casino is also conveniently located right near other major Baltimore attractions. Baltimore's sports complex, inner harbor, and famous sites such as The Hard Rock Cafe, The National Aquarium and Ripley's Believe it or Not Museum are all nestled in a tourist-friendly area and an excellent side trip from Annapolis. Another large casino and hotel are located in Arundel Mills, also about 30 minutes from Annapolis. Maryland Live! is a large complex situated next to the Arundel Mills Mall. The casino boasts an impressive list of entertainers each year!

The mall is home to a Medieval Times, an IMAX theater, plenty of shopping, and some fantastic restaurants of their own. My personal favorites are Zin Burger and Dave and Buster's. Zin Burger offers one of a kind, not to be rivaled, burgers, and handcrafted milkshakes. My personal recommendations are the Kobe Burger and the Chocolate Covered Pretzel milkshake. Dave and Buster's is fun for the kids and grownups alike. If you are not familiar with the restaurant, think Chuck E. Cheese but with an open bar and games for adults!

15. THE MARYLAND RENAISSANCE FESTIVAL

Maryland's famous Renaissance Festival is held just minutes from Annapolis each year from the end of August through the beginning of November. A Henry the Eighth themed festival, complete with the king himself, is sure to delight visitors of all ages. From jousting contests to archery to comedic performances and ale, lots, and lots of ale, it is a day full of entertainment. The Renn Fest, as it is referred to locally, attracts several of the same visitors every weekend. Many who design and sew their own costumes. A close friend of mine and theatrical costumer creates new dresses and garb each year. Going to see the beautiful and ornate costumes is part of the fun! The festival is held almost entirely outside, so plan for various weather. If it has rained recently, expect muddy and messy grounds.

SHOPPING & FUN!

16. A POTTER'S DELIGHT

The Annapolis Pottery, located on State Circle, is a delightful, winding store full of handmade goods and adorable souvenirs. It is a great place to lose yourself for half an hour or more. I often stop here when I need a gift for someone as it is a place to find original and unique pieces. You can find something for everyone here from handmade one of kind mugs to Maryland Crab style dishes, Christmas ornaments, and décor. The Annapolis Pottery has been in the same building since its founding in 1969.

17. BOOKS GLORIOUS BOOKS

Downtown is host to several delightful bookstores that are sure to provide you with the old-world charm you are looking for while visiting. On Main Street is the Back Creek Bookstore, which sells used books. Most of the books here are non-fiction and tend towards the historical. It also sells some collectible items and shelves a small fiction section. Located on the other side of State Circle, situated on Maryland Avenue, is Old Fox Books. A personal favorite of mine, it'll have you believing that Harry Potter and his friends could be found hanging out amongst the shelves. The store also boasts a coffee shop that serves up delicious brews. Make sure to check their events calendar for story hour and author meet and greets. The Annapolis Bookstore, located on Maryland Avenue, is a delightful little shop that sells new, used, and antique books. Comic and manga lovers Annapolis has you covered too! Head over to Capital Comics on Main Street to geek out. It is a small but well-stocked store with a friendly and knowledgeable staff.

18. ANNAPOLIS TOWN CENTER

The Town Center is a great place to do some more mainstream shopping. The anchor store is a Target, but it also is home to Whole Foods, Anthropologie, Paper House, Lou Lou, and Aarhus, to name a few.

My favorite two places in the complex are BIN201 and Paladar. BIN201 a fantastic wine shop with vintages galore. Their staff is extremely knowledgeable and helpful, so whether you are seeking a $15 bottle or a $500 bottle, they have you covered. In the back of the shop, they have a small craft beer section, and they also stock liqueurs and liquors, including some harder to find options. They host regular wine tastings, classes, and events, so be sure to check their website for their most current happenings. I personally recommend buying their monthly case of mixed wine for some great wine at a terrific price. BIN201 often offers prizes in their cases, especially around the holidays, and one year I won a $400 bottle! Paladar is a Latin Kitchen and Rum Bar with unique craft cocktails and fabulous food. Taco Tuesday is a great night to check out Paladar! I also recommend their rum-glazed Cuban pork and the wild salmon sockeye and spinach salad. Paladar has a small patio section for outdoor seating, as well as an expansive bar area. The town center is roughly a five-minute drive from downtown and offers free parking. There are three garages and one parking lot.

19. WESTFIELD ANNAPOLIS

Westfield Mall is the place to go if you are looking for retail galore. This massive shopping mall has pretty much every store you can think of, and probably a few you did not! One of my favorites in the geek-themed store BoxLunch. It is owned by the same company as Hot Topic but caters to a more mature crowd. An additional bonus is that BoxLunch donates $10 of every sale to help feed America's homeless. There are only 50 of these stores nationwide, making their merchandise much coveted by geeks and nerds alike! From Disney to Harry Potter to Anime, they have you covered. You'll also want to stop by Kokee Tea and grab one of their creative and delicious bubble teas or smoothies. Westfield boasts restaurants galore and has an impressive and recently modernized food court. Several popular restaurants surround the mall, including Uncle Julio's, Applebee's, and Red Lobster. The mall even hosts a small branch of the Anne Arundel County Library and a fantastic children's play space called Be With Me: The Children's Playseum. Lastly, the mall is home to an IMAX movie theater for a night at the movies!

20. ANNAPOLIS HARBOR CENTER

Annapolis Harbor Center is one of my favorite places to go on a beautiful day. It is an and outdoor styled center with many familiar shops and amenities. The Yankee Candle Shop and Bath & Body Works are two of my favorites. Additionally, there is a movie theater and a natural food market. The center's highlight is the Amish Market, an indoor farmers market covering almost 300,000 square feet. The market is open Thursdays, Fridays, and Saturdays and houses the Dutch Market Restaurant open all three days at 8am for breakfast. Adjacent to the market is a deck area great for little kids to run off some energy. The center often hosts events that utilize their outdoor space, so make sure to check their events calendar! Their Halloween themed Fall Fest has always been a favorite of my children.

TOURS & CRAWLS

21. PIRATE BOAT TOURS

Pirate tours are a must if you have kids. Pirate Adventures on the Chesapeake offers the chance for your little one to dress up as a pirate and zoom around the bay searching for treasure. Mayhap, mischief, and fun are guaranteed. The tour takes your children around the bay looking for the infamous pirate that stole your treasure. Once located, kids have the opportunity to knock down this devious thief using water cannons. Each little pirate leaves with a bag full of richness and goodies. Your tour guide will make sure that the adults have just as much fun as the kids!

22. GHOST TOURS

Annapolis, like many other cities rich in History, has delightful ghost tours. Haunted Harbor Tours provides the darker side of Annapolis lore researched and pulled from historical documents and newspaper clippings. Annapolis Tours and Crawls offers a walking ghost tour which provides you with some chilling facts about Annapolis history while visiting the city's most haunted sites! Annapolis Tours and

Crawls also offers a Haunted Pub tour providing you with spirits of both the otherworldly and drinkable kind. If you feel like making the 40-minute drive to Baltimore while visiting, they also offer a Haunted Pub Tour of Fells Point. Baltimore shares a rich and haunted history with many ties to Annapolis.

23. HISTORICAL TOURS

Historical tours are prevalent in the Annapolis area, with so much History that probably comes as no surprise. Annapolis Tours and Crawls offers a Twisted History walking tour and a Twisted History Pub Crawl, sharing some fun, engaging, and unique facts about Annapolis.

Annapolis Tours by Watermark provides knowledgeable hosts dressed in colonial garb. This tour company presents you with an enjoyable and easy-paced tour around downtown. These daytime tours offer you a myriad of facts and the opportunity to learn about Annapolis and its history from the experts.

24. PUB CRAWLS & FOOD TOURS

Annapolis is an excellent place to partake in pub crawls and food tours. Given the diverse options available, there is sure to be a crawl to fit everyone's tastes! Annapolis Food Tours offers you a walk-through history along with providing some delicious food. In addition to the food and drinks, they make stops a few notable historical sites in the city and provide historical context. They also offer the Ultimate Pub Crawl, which guarantees you 5 delicious drinks and three small plate offerings along the way! You will 3-6 local pubs, and the tours are offered evenings, weekends and during happy hour. "Murder, mayhem, sex. Scandal and local drunk history!" is how Annapolis Tours & Crawls describes their twisted history pub crawl. This fun and unique tour are guaranteed to satiate the history lover and drink lover combined.

25. COUNT DE ROCHAMBEAU HOUSE

Hamilton, The Broadway musical, took the world by storm a few years ago. The Annapolis area is one of the best places to experience some of the historical sites associated with the American Revolution. On your way out of Annapolis on General's Highway is the home that was part of the plantation Lafayette and his troops camped on as they traveled to meet Washington at Mt. Vernon. The 8.06 mile stretch of road is named General's Highway because it is the road on which Washington traveled to Annapolis to resign his military commission. It is a modest pale-yellow house that sits slightly back from the road and probably wouldn't catch your attention unless you knew to look for it! The Maryland Historical Trust has posted sign markers all over the state, indicating famous roads and sites related to American History. You can visit their website for a full list of driving tours that are themed based. The site will provide you with map coordinates for each marker as well as a google map with location.

26. HISTORIC LONDON TOWN AND GARDENS

This delightful tourist location is like visiting a mini version of Williamsburg, VA. There are beautiful gardens to wander through, and you can tour the William Brown House built circa 1760. They often host educational events for the family that include a lesson in history, often centered on what life was like for colonial children. Adult-themed events such as "Colonial Cocktails," during which you will be taught how to make two historic colonial drinks and get to enjoy them are also offered. They occasionally host evening concerts throughout the summer that are free of charge. Historic London Town hosts its very own colonial-themed escape room for groups of 4-10. Every December Historic London Town is decorated for Christmas. The event is called Illuminated London Town and is a delight for the whole family. Hot cider and smores roasting are two treats on offer. Additionally, you can stroll through the beautifully decorated gardens or participate in colonial festivities in the William Parker House, illuminated by candlelight. Parking is free year-round.

27. SANDY POINT PARK

Sandy Point State Park is the last stop before you hit the iconic Bay Bridge. The park boasts a beach you can swim at, but you should be aware, the sand is more like a pebble/gravel consistency, not that of a typical beach. They offer picnic areas with a view of the Chesapeake Bay as well as grills to prep food on. There are public restrooms available and concessions, but I recommend you bring your own food. This is an excellent place for small children to play and swim due to the lack of waves and shallow waters. Dogs are welcome, and they even have an area specifically for the dogs to swim. There is a parking fee, and it varies depending on the time of year. Fees are slightly higher for out of state residents, so please check before arriving. During the holiday season, they have a delightful light display you can drive through. The cost is roughly $15 per car, but you can typically find discounted coupons if you look online.

28. THE BAY BRIDGE

While a bridge may seem an odd thing to highlight, the Bay Bridge is an iconic Maryland symbol just west of Annapolis that connects Maryland's eastern and western shores. When the original bridge opened in 1952, it was 4.3 miles (6.9km), and it was the longest continuous over-water steel structure. An additional side was added in 1973 to accommodate increased traffic flow. It is worth the small toll to drive over, especially if the weather is clear or blue or a beautiful sunset. Once you get to the other side, there are a series of great restaurants where you can eat and enjoy a view of the bay. The first Sunday in May used to be the Bay Bridge Walk allowing pedestrians to walk the 4.5-mile span. In recent history, due to construction, it has been canceled and replaced with the Across the Bay 10k. You can visit the race website for more information.

UNIQUE SPOTS

29. GRAUL'S GROCERY

A grocery store may seem like an odd thing to add to a tourist tip list, but there is something special about Graul's. Graul's has been a staple in the Annapolis community since 1958. The original store was opened in Baltimore in 1920. It is a 4th generation family run business, and you can feel that in the store's atmosphere. Personal family recipes stock the shelves along with more familiar brand items. I highly recommend a visit to their bakery where items are baked fresh daily. My favorite is donuts! They have a second, smaller location at Cape St. Claire.

30. DESIGNATED HISTORICAL HOUSES

One of the many things I love about Annapolis is the designated historic homes throughout the city. I enjoy walking around and just looking at them and taking them in. My favorite street is Fleet Street, an almost alley-like road lined on both sides by houses that hold this designation. The homes on the Fleet Street are not the grand mansions and estates, but more the average family homes that people still live in today. I love to approach the harbor by walking down this small, brightly colored street that still holds on to that colonial charm. Almost anywhere you wander in Annapolis, you are sure to come across these beautiful pieces of History. They are marked by a small bronze plaque on the wall of the home.

31. FAMOUS HOMES

If you love to tour and see old homes and want to see Annapolis's grander side, here is the list for you. Many famous names from history resided here, and many of the homes are available to visit and tour. I recommend the William Paca House & Garden, Hammond-Harwood House, and Historic Annapolis Inc. Each house has different policies on visiting, hours, and fees, so please check out their websites before arriving. A simple walking app on your phone is all you need to find these and many more to visit and see. If you download the app GPSMYCITY, you can enjoy a self-guided tour of ten of the city's most famous homes. The walk will take you approximately one hour to complete and covers 1 mile.

32. THERE IS A VERY OLD CANNON

On the grounds of the State Building is an English cannon that was brought over in 1634 and used for defense on the Fort at Old St. Mary's. At some point, it sunk to the bottom of the St. Mary River and was subsequently recovered in 1822. Currently, the cannon resides on the lawn of the Maryland State House, and you can walk right up and touch it. The cannon has been on display since 1908 and is a small but neat piece of Maryland and early American History. The surrounding grounds of the Maryland State House are a great place to relax and for kids to run around in the grass. There are benches and plush grass, so a picnic is a great option!

PLACES TO STAY

33. THE ANNAPOLIS INN

If you are looking for a room to stay with that old-fashioned historical feel and elegance, then The Annapolis Inn is your place to go. The rooms are gorgeously outfitted in Georgian-era style. The B&B is situated in the heart of downtown and offers free breakfast and free Wi-Fi. Room rates can peak, especially during the summer tourist season, however, if elegance and being draped in history are your goals, then this is the place to retreat. The B&B is located at 144 Prince George Street.

34. THE FLAG HOUSE INN

This B&B delivers old-world charm at affordable rates. The rooms are delightfully decorated, and some offer a separate sitting area. The colorful Victorian-style rooms offer that old-world charm many who venture to Annapolis are seeking. Each room has its own unique theme ranging from nautical to floral to British imperial. Rooms have a private bathroom, flatscreen T.V., and views of the city. They offer a free breakfast, a beautiful common area, free Wi-Fi, and free parking. They also provide a free airport shuttle. The B&B is located at 124 Randall St.

35. THE INN AT HORN POINT

Located on the Eastport side of Annapolis, this charming little inn is a beautiful and quiet spot to book your stay. The Inn at Horn Point offers free breakfast, seven days a week. Monday through Friday is a large continental, and on the weekends, they offer a full three-course gourmet meal. This well-kept inn offers five delightful rooms. Each one is named for a famous yacht designed and built by Johnny Trumpy, the renowned shipbuilder, whose home the B&B used to be. Flatscreen T.V.'s and free Wi-Fi are included in each room. The inn has free parking available in their driveway and on the street outside. Horn Point does not permit children under the age of 13 unless your party has reserved the entire Inn for your stay. The inn is located at 100 Chesapeake Ave.

36. MAINSTREAM HOTEL OPTIONS

There are bed and breakfasts galore in Annapolis that range widely in cost and amenities. If a mainstream hotel is more your style, you will most likely have to venture out of downtown. The two options that are downtown are the Annapolis Waterfront Hotel and the Hilton Garden Inn. Located just outside of the city-center on West Street is the Westin Annapolis. If you have a car or don't mind using a service like Uber or Lyft to get you downtown and back, you have several options. There are mainstream hotels near the Annapolis Town Center and the Annapolis Harbor Center only 1-2 miles outside of downtown. These will cost you about half the price as a stay city-center, averaging around $85-$150 a night. County Inn & Suites, Crowne Plaza, Best Western, Holiday Inn Express, Doubletree, Courtyard by Marriott are just a few of the options you will have.

BARS, COFFEE, AND DELICIOUS FOOD!

37. SPEAKEASIES

Prohibition vibe bars are always a fun place to hang and experience an array of handmade cocktails. Dry85, located on Main Street, is a favorite of mine. While the food is good, this is a place you go for the drinks. The Lavender Field's of Kentucky is my go-to. Made with Knob Creek Bourbon, house-made lavender vanilla bean syrup, freshly squeezed lime, and topped with ginger ale. They offer whiskey flights for every price point and an extensive bourbon, scotch, rye, and whiskey menu. The Fox's Den, also located on Main street, is easy to miss as it is wedged down a set of stairs between two retail shops at 179b Main Street. Typically, an advertising sandwich board or a bouncer to check I.D.'s is located on the sidewalk to help you discover this prohibition-style pub. Once you venture down to this basement bar, you will not be disappointed. Rustic and screaming of backroom prohibition, it's a great spot to grab some drinks and food.

38. CAFES AND COFFEE SHOPS

Coffee shops and cafes abound in Annapolis so here is my take on the top shops. City Dock Coffee makes delicious coffee and drinks and has one location right on the waterfront. City Dock also has a location on Maryland Ave. (both offer a restroom for customers!). It has that indie coffee-shop vibe and is a great place to sit and relax. The location on Maryland Ave. is significantly smaller than the waterfront local, so if you are planning to sit inside and relax, I recommend you head further downtown. Around the corner from City Dock on Main Street, you have a Starbucks, which is always a favorite of mine and a familiar go-to. It offers a unique nautical theme and a beautiful mural inside on the left as you walk through the door. The best perk about Starbucks is public restrooms. If you walk to the top of Main Street (it's a hill), you will come upon The Red Bean, which sells not only delicious coffee but ice cream! Blackberry green tea and mango rum pineapple are two of the delicious ice cream flavors on offer.

39. THE REYNOLD'S TAVERN

This restaurant is a thriving piece of Annapolis history. The pub was the original kitchen and hat shop of William Reynolds and was built in 1737. It still has original brick floors, walls, fireplace, and a stairwell from the initial construction. The tavern is a designated historical landmark. You can enjoy a full tea service, an elegant dinner in the main dining room, or a relaxed evening in their outdoor beer garden. The tea rooms on the first floor have been well preserved and look remarkably like how they were initially designed. The tavern also has a few hotel rooms should you want to stay and eat there. There are so many fantastic options on the menu. Some items change seasonally, but I recommend the 1747 fries coated in rosemary, truffle oil, garlic and parmesan, and the warm goat cheese salad, which is served with brandied blueberries and candied pecans.

The Reynold's Tavern is a way to enjoy dining inside a piece of history.

40. THE HIDEAWAY

One of my favorite restaurants in Maryland is outside of Annapolis. Roughly a 25-minute drive northwest of the city, you will find The Hideaway, or maybe you won't, I drove past it the first time! The name fits the location because it is tucked on a back road in Odenton, MD, and fashioned out of an old home. If you love BBQ, beer, and whiskey, then this is the place to go. Their dry-rubbed hot wings served with blackberry chipotle is ordered every time I go. If you are looking for authentic and top-notch Maryland, Crab Soup look no further. From ribs to chicken potpie to pork BBQ, The Hideaway has you covered. Tuesday night wine bottles are half off, and while it is not an extensive selection, half off is hard to beat! No matter what you chose to eat, you will be satisfied, just make sure to leave room for some homemade ice cream for dessert!

41. LOBSTER ROLLS

Usually, when one thinks of Maryland, they think crabs, and they're not wrong, but situated on Main Street in Annapolis is Mason's Famous Lobster Rolls. There are six delicious options and a variety of sides and soft drinks to complete your meal. Many people state they can't visit Annapolis without having one these, indeed, famous rolls. Other entrees include salads, lobster bisque, and lobster mac n' cheese. It is the perfect lunch spot to take a break from walking and sightseeing.

42. ALL YOU CAN EAT SEAFOOD

Buddy's Crabs and Ribs located in downtown Annapolis is a great place to go for some all you can eat seafood! The buffet offers various types of shrimp, fish, oysters, mussels, chicken, vegetables, and more. It also has an extensive menu to order from, fresh steamed crabs by the dozen and a full bar. The restaurant faces the harbor, so if you are lucky, you will get a waterfront table while you dine. The dessert bar is almost as large as the buffet, so leave some room to try at least a few delicious bites. I enjoy the cream puffs! Kids under 5 eat free and kids 6-12 are half price. This is a great place to eat if you have a large group, have time to kill, or desire to take your time over a leisurely meal. Be sure to check out their merchandise before you leave!

43. RED, RED WINE

Wine lovers rejoice! Red, Red Wine has one of the most extensive wine lists I have ever seen. I have discovered many wines here that I have then purchased for home consumption. They offer a variety of wine flights, wine by the glass, and of course, wine by the bottle. If you enjoy a bright red, I recommend Oregon Trails Wine Company's Pinot Noir. I first had this wine as part of a flight and order it frequently when I come here. This restaurant is special to me for personal reasons, but it is the food and the wine I keep returning for. I recommend one of their flatbreads or checking out their New Orleans style brunch on Sundays and ordering the Crab Benedict or the Bayou Breakfast Burger. The food menu is not as extensive as the drink, and wine menu, so picky eaters and kids may not find this place as exciting as adults. In the evenings, this is a fantastic spot for a romantic date and quiet conversation. Red,

Red Wine is not a spot frequented by the bar-hopping crowd unless a theater cast has taken up the tables outside, which we have! Therefore, it is a fantastic spot to sit inside at the bar and relax. When the weather is nice, I enjoy sitting out on the patio and participating in some excellent people (and dog) watching!

44. THE BEST MARGARITAS AND TACOS

Vida is the place to go for the BEST tacos and margaritas I have ever had. Everything is made fresh daily, and the margaritas are spot on. You can order by the glass or by the pitcher. As a margarita lover, I was skeptical when my partner told these were the best, but I am happy to say he was correct! In addition to the house margarita, I recommend the spicy margarita or the seasonal watermelon margarita. My favorite taco is the scallop taco, but honestly, I have tried them all, and you cannot go wrong. The Brussel sprout side is another favorite of mine, as well as their queso dip. Tuesdays you receive 20% off the check and Sundays house margaritas are $5. You order per taco and can order in waves, so bring your appetite and prepare for a fabulous night of food!

45. SUSHI

Maryland is the place for seafood, as we are surrounded by water. Sushi places abound, so it can be hard to figure which are top-notch and which to avoid. My personal favorite is Tsunami located on West Street. Every day has a different special, so check the daily deal online.

The best bang for your buck is Sundays when they offer half-off EVERY roll until 7:30pm. If you are not a sushi lover, have no fear other delicious options include the Buddha Bowl and Lobster Mac n Cheese. Tsunami can become very busy, so I recommend you make a reservation. Other popular Sushi joints are Joss Café, Osteria, and another favorite of mine, Nano Asian Dining; all three are located on Main Street. Joss Cafe and Osteria are upscale dining, while Nano Asian Dining is down to earth, delicious food.

46. HARRY BROWNE'S

An art deco dining room and old-time bar featured upstairs; Harry Browne's is an Annapolis staple. The late-night weekend bar crowd usually consists of local actors post-show. Frequently on Friday evenings, it will play host to staged readings from the local theater The Colonial Players. The dining room caters to long-time Annapolis natives, think old money, and workers from the capitol building during the week lunch rush. That, however, should not stop you from enjoying this Annapolis tradition/ Their Sunday brunch is delicious, and the mimosas are spot on. Pack your Sunday best if you plan to eat in the dining room.

47. SMALL PLATES THAT MEASURE UP

Level: A Small Plates Lounge is one of my favorite places for a date night with my guy. Hands down, the BEST food in Annapolis. Their ever-revolving farm to table seasonal menu will not leave you disappointed. Combine that with handcrafted cocktails, many that change regularly, and you are guaranteed a night of gastro delight. They do not post their dinner menu on their site because of how frequently it changes, but they do offer a list of drinks always available at the bar. My two personal favorites are the Level Gimlet and the Angels and Demons. The gimlet has a fantastic lime foam on top, and the Angels and Demons is created with Jimador Tequila, St. Germaine, agave habanero, and micro cilantro.

Because of Level's interior design, it can be VERY noisy, so this is not the place to go for a quiet and intimate conversation. Their dress code is smart casual, and they ask that gentlemen refrain from wearing sports jerseys or sleeveless shirts. Small plates do not mean a small bill, but if you go in knowing that I assure you, it is worth the price! Level opens at 4pm daily, and a reservation is recommended.

48. FARM TO TABLE

If you love Farm to Table restaurants as I do, then Annapolis is a great place to eat. My personal favorite is Preserve, located on Main Street. It has large barn door windows that open on beautiful days, which gives you the feeling of being outside. Their menu changes regularly, so there is always something new to try. The name Preserve comes from the owners' love of pickling, fermenting, and preserving foods and menus of these tasty options are featured on the menu. They offer a pickled appetizer with three of their house-made pickled vegetable options. Preserve is closed on Mondays and closes between 3pm and 5pm each day. Another hot spot is Vin909, located on the East Port side of Annapolis. They source many of their ingredients locally, and everything is prepared fresh. It is a small, cozy place, so not ideal for young children, especially since they do not accept reservations and are often busy. You may find yourself waiting a bit if you wish to dine here, so plan ahead and allow for plenty of time before your next scheduled activity.

49. FRESH CRABS

Maryland is the place for fresh crabs. Crab season runs from April to November, with the bigger and fatter crabs later in the fall. There are more places than I could count that offer fresh, delicious fresh steamed crabs, so I will just highlight a few. I encourage visitors to the Annapolis area to do their own research on this subject, especially since there are so many choices. Additionally, if you have never picked crabs before, yes the expression is picking crabs because you literally pick them apart, I have included a resource at the end of the book to learn the ins and outs. My first recommendation is Mike's Restaurant & Crabhouse, roughly a 15-minute drive from downtown Annapolis in Riva, MD. It sits on the water, boasts a sizeable outdoor deck, and offers delicious food. Second is Cantler's Riverside Inn in Annapolis, about 2 miles away from the Naval Academy. Cantler's is situated on the water and offers many tables outside on their deck. Both restaurants are owned by Maryland residents and provide a friendly, family atmosphere. Eating steamed crabs is a messy affair, so don't wear your nicest clothes when you head out!

50. COOPER'S HAWK

Located at the Annapolis Town Center, Cooper's Hawk is a beautiful restaurant and winery. Their menu boasts some of the most delicious food I have had in the area, and I love that they have a key on their menu to pair their food with their wines. It is the perfect spot for a romantic date or a Sunday brunch with the family. They have a beautiful second-story patio for when the weather is excellent as well. I have eaten both inside and outside and have loved it every time.

ADDITIONAL SERVICES/TIPS

There is a decent-sized CVS on the main street if you need some of the staple items. I would recommend picking up additional sunscreen, sunglasses, etc. here as they won't be as pricey as some of the tourist shops. CVS is the only mainstream convenience store within walking distance of downtown and has a pharmacy on site. The store is open 8am - 10pm Monday through Saturday and 10 am to 8 pm on Sunday. Please note, the pharmacy's hours are different from the store and closed on Sunday.

BONUS TIP 1: ANNE ARUNDEL MEDICAL CENTER

Should you require emergency medical care during your visit, the Anne Arundel Medical Center is one of the best hospitals in Maryland. It is a state-of-the-art hospital that almost feels like a resort hotel with all the shops and amenities. On a handful of occasions, my family has needed emergency treatment for stitches, appendicitis, and a kidney infection. We have chosen to go there because we knew we would receive 5-star medical treatment. The doctors and nurses are kind, knowledgeable, and helpful. They had a dedicated children's emergency room decorated as if you were in an underwater adventure to provide a soothing experience for you and your little one.

BONUS TIP 2: PARKING DOWNTOWN

There are two places I recommend for parking downtown. The first is the Calvert Street Garage. During the day, this garage is reserved for government employees but weeknights at 6, and every weekend this large garage is open free to the public. It will add a few minutes of walking, depending on where you are headed, but not much. If you are headed to West Street, this a great spot to park. The garage is located at 19 St Johns St, Annapolis, MD 21401. The other option I use when Calvert is not open to the public is Gott's Court Garage. The parking rates are exceptionally low and a great option if you must pay to park. It is located at 25 Calvert St, Annapolis, MD 21401. If you really do not mind dealing with Main Street traffic, one-way roads, and pedestrians, you can try the Noah Hillman Parking garage. This place is often full and busy on event days and can be an annoyance to get out of since it lets out directly on Main Street. The rate at publishing was $20/day. It is located at 150 Gorman St, Annapolis, MD 21401.

With so much to do in Annapolis, I recommend making a list of your top ten must-and-or-or-see items. Tours, Trivia Nights, Pub Crawls, and Karaoke all have fluctuating schedules, so it is recommended to call ahead.

Steamed crab prices vary in market price based on size. Average prices range anywhere from $30 for a dozen male #2's, the smallest size, to well over $100 per dozen. A dozen regular small to medium crabs is perfect for two people if you are adding traditional sides such as hush puppies, steamed corn, and shrimp.

The Annapolis bar scene is animated at nights and especially in the spring and summer weekends. Most locales will check your I.D. before permitting entry, so make sure you have it on you. I have been asked for I.D. many times, and I am well removed from 21!

If relaxing and sightseeing is your goal, I recommend that you check Annapolis tourist sites for peak times for events you may wish to avoid. Significant dates corresponding to the Naval

Academy, boat shows, or other festivals make Annapolis very busy and congested.

Downtown Annapolis is a fantastic spot, and you can easily fill a long weekend with sightseeing, tours, and gastro delights. Still, I recommend traveling out into the surrounding area of Anne Arundel County. Anne Arundel County offers a wide range of activities, shopping, entertainment, and beaches, so it is worthwhile to venture beyond the city's borders. Anne Arundel County is home to the Maryland Renaissance Festival held on weekends every fall.

TOP REASONS TO BOOK THIS TRIP

History: Annapolis is a city immersed in America's past.

Cuisine: Some of the best restaurants in Maryland are located here.

Water: From boating to beaches to scenic views.

DID YOU KNOW?

Four residents of Annapolis signed the original Declaration of Independence: William Paca, Samuel Chase, Charles Carroll, and Thomas Stone.

Pat Sajak, the Wheel of Fortune host, lives primarily in Anne Arundel Country, where Annapolis is situated. He was a significant benefactor to the Anne Arundel Medical Center, in Annapolis, during its remodeling. He and his wife were married in a church in Annapolis.

Annapolis was formed as a Puritan settlement by religious exiles from nearby Virginia.

Annapolis averages over 4,000 million visitors annually.

Annapolis was briefly the capital of the United States.

Congress was in session in the statehouse from November 26, 1783, to June 3, 1784. Its brief stint as capitol began after the signing of the Treaty of Paris.

OTHER RESOURCES:

Crab Picking Tips – Check out the Washington Post article "Crab Picking 10: Everything you wanted to know but was afraid to ask"

Annapolis.gov

annapolis.com

rennfest.com

downtownannapolis.org

baydreaming.com

chesapeakebay.net

TRIVIA

1) In what year was Annapolis founded?

2) What was the city's original name?

3) How many miles of shoreline does Anne Arundel County have?

4) How many boats are there in Anne Arundel County?

5) What part of infamous history did Annapolis play a key role in?

6) What is Annapolis, the capital of (besides Maryland)?

7) What famous fire movie was filmed mainly in Baltimore and Annapolis?

8) What is the city's annual revenue for tourism?

9) How many square miles is the surface of the Chesapeake Bay?

10) How many species of plants and animals live in the Chesapeake Bay?

ANSWERS

1) 1649

2) Providence

3) 533

4) Roughly 35,000

5) It was a major port for slavery until Maryland abolished it in 1864

6) It is called The Sailing Capital of the World

7) Ladder 49

8) $3.5 billion

9) 4,480 square miles

10) 3,600

PACKING AND PLANNING TIPS

A Week before Leaving

- Arrange for someone to take care of pets and water plants.
- Email and Print important Documents.
- Get Visa and vaccines if needed.
- Check for travel warnings.
- Stop mail and newspaper.
- Notify Credit Card companies where you are going.
- Passports and photo identification is up to date.
- Pay bills.
- Copy important items and download travel Apps.
- Start collecting small bills for tips.
- Have post office hold mail while you are away.
- Check weather for the week.
- Car inspected, oil is changed, and tires have the correct pressure.
- Check airline luggage restrictions.
- Download Apps needed for your trip.

Right Before Leaving

- Contact bank and credit cards to tell them your location.
- Clean out refrigerator.
- Empty garbage cans.
- Lock windows.
- Make sure you have the proper identification with you.
- Bring cash for tips.
- Remember travel documents.
- Lock door behind you.
- Remember wallet.
- Unplug items in house and pack chargers.
- Change your thermostat settings.
- Charge electronics, and prepare camera memory cards.

READ OTHER GREATER THAN A TOURIST BOOKS

Greater Than a Tourist- Geneva Switzerland: 50 Travel Tips from a Local by Amalia Kartika

Greater Than a Tourist- St. Croix US Birgin Islands USA: 50 Travel Tips from a Local by Tracy Birdsall

Greater Than a Tourist- San Juan Puerto Rico: 50 Travel Tips from a Local by Melissa Tait

Greater Than a Tourist – Lake George Area New York USA: 50 Travel Tips from a Local by Janine Hirschklau

Greater Than a Tourist – Monterey California United States: 50 Travel Tips from a Local by Katie Begley

Greater Than a Tourist – Chanai Crete Greece: 50 Travel Tips from a Local by Dimitra Papagrigoraki

Greater Than a Tourist – The Garden Route Western Cape Province South Africa: 50 Travel Tips from a Local by Li-Anne McGregor van Aardt

Greater Than a Tourist – Sevilla Andalusia Spain: 50 Travel Tips from a Local by Gabi Gazon

Children's Book: *Charlie the Cavalier Travels the World* by Lisa Rusczyk Ed. D.

> TOURIST

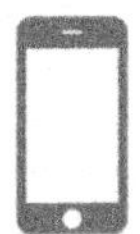

Follow us on Instagram for beautiful travel images:

http://Instagram.com/GreaterThanATourist

Follow *Greater Than a Tourist* on Amazon.

>Tourist Podcast

>T Website

>T Youtube

>T Facebook

>T Goodreads

>T Amazon

>T Mailing List

>T Pinterest

>T Instagram

>T Twitter

>T SoundCloud

>T LinkedIn

>T Map

> TOURIST

At *Greater Than a Tourist*, we love to share travel tips with you. How did we do? What guidance do you have for how we can give you better advice for your next trip? Please send your feedback to GreaterThanaTourist@gmail.com as we continue to improve the series. We appreciate your constructive feedback. Thank you.

METRIC CONVERSIONS

TEMPERATURE

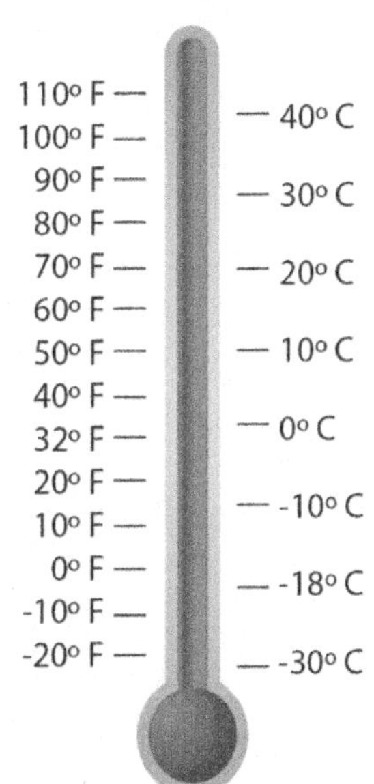

To convert F to C:

Subtract 32, and then multiply by 5/9 or .5555.

To Convert C to F:

Multiply by 1.8 and then add 32.

32F = 0C

LIQUID VOLUME

To Convert:....................Multiply by

U.S. Gallons to Liters................. 3.8

U.S. Liters to Gallons 26

Imperial Gallons to U.S. Gallons 1.2

Imperial Gallons to Liters....... 4.55

Liters to Imperial Gallons 22

1 Liter = .26 U.S. Gallon

1 U.S. Gallon = 3.8 Liters

DISTANCE

To convert ....Multiply by

Inches to Centimeters 2.54

Centimeters to Inches 39

Feet to Meters....................... .3

Meters to Feet 3.28

Yards to Meters 91

Meters to Yards 1.09

Miles to Kilometers 1.61

Kilometers to Miles............ .62

1 Mile = 1.6 km

1 km = .62 Miles

WEIGHT

1 Ounce = .28 Grams

1 Pound = .4555 Kilograms

1 Gram = .04 Ounce

1 Kilogram = 2.2 Pounds

TRAVEL QUESTIONS

- Do you bring presents home to family or friends after a vacation?
- Do you get motion sick?
- Do you have a favorite billboard?
- Do you know what to do if there is a flat tire?
- Do you like a sun roof open?
- Do you like to eat in the car?
- Do you like to wear sun glasses in the car?
- Do you like toppings on your ice cream?
- Do you use public bathrooms?
- Did you bring a cell phone and does it have power?
- Do you have a form of identification with you?
- Have you ever been pulled over by a cop?
- Have you ever given money to a stranger on a road trip?
- Have you ever taken a road trip with animals?
- Have you ever gone on a vacation alone?
- Have you ever run out of gas?

- If you could move to any place in the world, where would it be?
- If you could travel anywhere in the world, where would you travel?
- If you could travel in any vehicle, which one would it be?
- If you had three things to wish for from a magic genie, what would they be?
- If you have a driver's license, how many times did it take you to pass the test?
- What are you the most afraid of on vacation?
- What do you want to get away from the most when you are on vacation?
- What foods smell bad to you?
- What item do you bring on ever trip with you away from home?
- What makes you sleepy?
- What song would you love to hear on the radio when you're cruising on the highway?
- What travel job would you want the least?
- What will you miss most while you are away from home?
- What is something you always wanted to try?

- What is the best road side attraction that you ever saw?
- What is the farthest distance you ever biked?
- What is the farthest distance you ever walked?
- What is the weirdest thing you needed to buy while on vacation?
- What is your favorite candy?
- What is your favorite color car?
- What is your favorite family vacation?
- What is your favorite food?
- What is your favorite gas station drink or food?
- What is your favorite license plate design?
- What is your favorite restaurant?
- What is your favorite smell?
- What is your favorite song?
- What is your favorite sound that nature makes?
- What is your favorite thing to bring home from a vacation?
- What is your favorite vacation with friends?
- What is your favorite way to relax?
- Where is the farthest place you ever traveled in a car?

- Where is the farthest place you ever went North, South, East and West?
- Where is your favorite place in the world?
- Who is your favorite singer?
- Who taught you how to drive?
- Who will you miss the most while you are away?
- Who if the first person you will contact when you get to your destination?
- Who brought you on your first vacation?
- Who likes to travel the most in your life?
- Would you rather be hot or cold?
- Would you rather drive above, below, or at the speed limited?
- Would you rather drive on a highway or a back road?
- Would you rather go on a train or a boat?
- Would you rather go to the beach or the woods?

TRAVEL BUCKET LIST

1.

2.

3.

4.

5.

6.

7.

8.

9.

10.

NOTES

Made in the USA
Las Vegas, NV
30 April 2025

21517219R00059